TONGUES OF FIRE

PRAYERS THAT EXPOSE SECRET ENEMIES AND OPEN NEW DOORS

READ THIS.

Satan is the real enemy. He uses any available vessel to achieve his aim. People are not the enemy, Satan is. When you pray, you fight against evil forces and strip them of power and control.

Once the power behind every plot against you is taken away, nothing can harm you. In some cases, people that devil used become friends who could help you reach your goal. Since they knew how to stop you, they naturally can show you what you need to do to enjoy new opportunities.

As you pray these prayers with faith, focus on Satan and all his demonic activities. Your victory is sure in the name of Jesus Christ.

George C. Goodman

ONE

CANCEL EVIL PLANS

Luke 16:1-3

Jesus told this story to his disciples: "There was a certain rich man who had a manager handling his affairs. One day a report came that the manager was wasting his employer's money. So the employer called him in and said, 'What's this I hear about you? Get your report in order, because you are going to be fired.' "The manager thought to himself, 'Now what? My boss has fired me. I don't have the strength to dig ditches, and I'm too proud to beg.

The careless steward got carried away by his position in his master's business. He gave out his master's goods more than necessary. This gave his enemies an advantage due to his careless attitude to work and almost ruined his entire life. The people he gave those goods might have been happy to put him in that mess. But the servant did not know about their secret plan. He must have forgotten about it until his master called him to give an account of his service.

The fact about life is that once we have some form of promotion, we become less careful of dangers. We slide back to a life of ease and convenience, thinking less of the sudden or subtle dangers

we may face. This comfort zone
is risky to us both in the short
and long term. This is where
many people stop praying,
fasting, and studying the word
of God. They forget that with
promotion comes persecution
and assaults from the enemy.
Perhaps, these and many more
were the experiences of the
man in the story.

He may not have received a
promotion but it is clear that he
had a special task and some
privileges higher than the other
servants in the service of his
master. People who didn't like
him want to ruin his career and
rob him of those privileges.
They planned to see him fail
woefully. Envy and jealousy got
the best of them and they could
not but seek his downfall. They

had only one aim: to disgrace him and make him a laughingstock before all the people that knew him.

Do you have a nice job but you don't seem to know what's making you sad and unfulfilled? Sometimes, it isn't because you have something higher to pursue. It could be that the enemy has decided to make your life miserable until you lose the things that mean a lot to you. You may have been getting attention from your boss. You may have been going on trips more than everyone in your organization.

There is no saying that everyone around is your enemy. But the fact is that the enemy, Satan, can use anyone to achieve his goals. One of his goals is to make sure that you don't have the good things of life. And if you do, the devil doesn't want you to enjoy it for too long. He is the devil, and that is what he is good at. You can't let your guard down at your moment of promotion and happiness.

New heights often attract new challenges; new levels new devils, and so it goes for everyone. And unless you begin to spend more time with God, study the Word, and pray as though your life depends on it, you may lose your juicy position before you know it. Do not think that there is a moment of rest on this earth. As long as we live, we will continue to wage a war against

the forces of darkness. Claim
your position in Christ and
release his blessings and
deliverance upon your life in
the name of Jesus.

PRAYER

Father, I declare that I will not
allow promotion, prosperity,
and achievements make me
careless, less prayerful, or lazy.
I receive the grace to take my
position in God through Christ
Jesus to live a life of discipline,
faith, and dependence on God. I
choose to make it a habit to
fast, pray and study the word of
God at all times. Lord, save me
from every secret plan of my
enemies in Jesus name. I
command all their plans to fail
in the name of Jesus.

TWO
EXPOSE THE SECRET ENEMY

Luke 16:1-2

Jesus told this story to his disciples: "There was a certain rich man who had a manager handling his affairs. One day a report came that the manager was wasting his employer's money. So the employer called him in and said, 'What's this I hear about you? Get your report in order, because you are going to be fired.'

Do you know that the bible didn't mention the identity of the people behind the misfortune of the steward? They were faceless enemies who, though unknown and unseen, destroyed everything he had worked hard for. The bible didn't even mention that the steward knew them or had expected something like that. Nevertheless, the secret plans of his enemies worked perfectly.

Your enemy may be anywhere and everywhere but that doesn't mean that you should live in fear. No, that would go against the will of God. God has given you a spirit of boldness and power. The people you pass on the streets may be the enemy. The people in the same workplace with you can be the enemy. There is no telling from who or where the next attack is coming. They could be family members, close friends, or coworkers. Whoever they are, you cannot afford to let down your guard, especially when they hang out with you.

From the story, the boss asked the servant to give an account of his business transactions and leave the job as well. The nature of his ordeal could mean that the enemy was within. They wanted to take his place once he is disgraced and let off his juicy position.

One thing you must keep in mind as you go about your daily duty is that no matter how good and decent people may look, envy and greed can reside in them. You need to be careful in everything you do if you would succeed and enjoy your success for a very long time. Your

faceless enemies are watching
your every move, and they will
strike when you are not
watchful.

PRAYER

Heavenly Father, expose all my
faceless enemies in the church,
family, business, and workplace
in the name of Jesus. I receive
the gift of discernment to
identify anyone who wants to
bring my downfall through
envy or greed. Let all their
plans fail in Jesus' name.

THREE
RECEIVE A GRACE PERIOD

Luke 16:2-8

So the employer called him in and said, 'What's this I hear about you? Get your report in order, because you are going to be fired.' "The manager thought to himself, 'Now what? My boss has fired me. I don't have the strength to dig ditches, and I'm too proud to beg. Ah, I know how to ensure that I'll have plenty of friends who will give me a home when I am fired.' "So he invited each person who owed money to his employer to come and discuss the situation. He asked the first one, 'How much do you owe him?' The man replied, 'I owe him 800 gallons of olive oil.' So the manager told him, 'Take the bill and quickly change it to 400 gallons. ' "'And how much do you owe my employer?' he asked the next man. 'I owe him 1,000 bushels of wheat,' was the reply. 'Here,' the manager said, 'take the bill and change it to 800 bushels. ' "The rich man had to admire the dishonest rascal for being so shrewd. And it is true that the children of this world are shrewder in dealing with the world around them than are the children of the light.

You may have noticed that the steward had some time to think of what to do after he was let off his precious job. This could mean that the master wasn't so mean to this servant. He may have given him enough time to think of his wrong decisions. The steward himself had some personal plans but these were disrupted by the seriousness of the matter at hand.

Yet he didn't give up and allow the unexpected misfortune to decide his future and happiness. He made sure he reversed his situation. He was going to have a better and bigger life no matter what the enemy thought they had done. The little time his boss gave him was a priceless gift. He used that opportunity to devise a plan B.

You may be experiencing something similar in your life. If you have fallen into a mess in your relationship, business, or job, I pray that a second chance is given to you. If you need a grace period to think about your life and make amends, God will grant your wish. Everyone deserves a second chance and you are not going to miss yours. When God does it for you, use that period to make a plan so great that your enemies will hide in shame.

PRAYER

Father, I ask you to give me a grace period for this problem that I face. Do not allow my enemies to destroy everything you have helped me accomplish in the church, family, business, and marriage. I declare that it is not too late to make a new beginning and I claim a grace period to regain and recover

everything in the name of
Jesus.

FOUR

NO ONE CAN LAY ME OFF

Luke 16:4
Ah, I know how to ensure that I'll have plenty of friends who will give me a home when I am fired.'

The intention of the enemies was revealed by the steward himself. They aimed to make sure he lost his job and position in the service of his master who happened to be a rich man. Although he seemed unable to identify the persons behind his ordeal, he nevertheless knew what they were up to. Luckily for him, he had resolved what to do when put out of active service.

Are there enemies trying to put you out and make sure you are laid off? While they are the physical faces behind the secret plan, Satan is the mastermind behind all the attacks. It is the practice of the Father-of-all-lies to bring accusations against God's people. No human being is exempted in the enemy's plot against all that is good and lovely.

Is there an obvious sign to put out the fire in your local church and your Christian life? If your prayer life is going down and you feel helpless, an enemy could be behind it. You cannot allow the conspiracies to continue. The world is changing and strange viruses are attacking the human race. These are not natural and they can never be. The enemy's target is to lay many people off, keep them penniless at home and make them consider the option of suicide.

You have a destiny; you are more than a living human. You are a child of God and you can't let the devil or enemies decide your life. Remember how the steward reversed his situation; you too can overturn the sinister plot of the enemy. Declare yourself exempted from layoffs by your organization in the name of Jesus.

PRAYER
Father, I ask that you reveal the plans of all my enemies and

expose them all. Wherever they have gathered to take my peace away, I ask, Lord, that you shield me from their evil plans in the name of Jesus. I declare your protection over my marriage, job, home, family, and business in the mighty name of Jesus.

FIVE

I HAVE A GOOD PLAN

Luke 16:3-5

"The manager thought to himself, 'Now what? My boss has fired me. I don't have the strength to dig ditches, and I'm too proud to beg. Ah, I know how to ensure that I'll have plenty of friends who will give me a home when I am fired.'
"So he invited each person who owed money to his employer to come and discuss the situation. He asked the first one, 'How much do you owe him?'

As we bring this interesting story to a close, it is helpful to realize that the steward was initially discouraged. He was so confused that he questioned his fate and was doubtful of the future. But then, he woke up from the sleep of defeat and despondency. He asked himself what to do, knowing that most times solutions come from within.

Many times, we look to people for solutions, forgetting that it isn't always the case. When you look inward, you will find what you are looking for. It may surprise you to discover hidden talents, skills, or opportunities you might have missed due to the position you occupied. Do not be in a hurry to get a quick fix from a friend or a former colleague. They may eventually come in handy but don't make them your first point of visit yet until the time is right.

Is your job on the line already and you do not know what to do? Is your marriage or business going down the drain and it seems nothing can save it? Before you make that next phone call, wait. You need to look away from people and look within. Jesus commended the servant for having the right mindset and for making the right move during a difficult moment.

The steward did what he had to do to save his job. He went around and met all the debtors and collected amounts that were lower than what they owed. Even though the master lost some money, he was able to get what we may consider as the cost price. This act may have saved his job and endeared him more to his master. Sometimes, you need to do all you can to save a part of a situation and not let everything fall apart.

PRAYER

Father, grant me supernatural wisdom to save the day. I receive divine wisdom to think right, act right, and speak right in the name of Jesus. Let the cloud of your glory follow me everywhere I go in the name of Jesus.

SIX

LET YOUR FIRE FALL

Luke 12:49
"I have come to set the world on fire, and I wish it were already burning!

Our Lord, Jesus Christ, had a mission of setting the world on fire. This was not a case of arson or an intention to destroy everything he created. He said that he did not come to destroy the law or the prophet. So he was talking about the fire of zeal, interest, and expectation. Without these forms of fire, you may go for days without a spark of life. Life becomes boring and weighs you down with many worries. Even the things you love – service to God, family, job – all becomes a heavy burden. Your commitment to important things is a measure of the level of fire you have. When you lack the desire to pray or to do things that will move you forward, danger waits at the corner.

Jesus must have noticed the coldness in the people who followed him before he made that remark. We are no different from the people of Jesus' days. We are down when all is not going well, and we are up when we live a comfortable life. Although this is a sign of being human, it is not supposed to be so. You must seek to rekindle the fire of God or else you remain below God's expectation for you. If you have stopped working voluntarily for your local assembly, it is time to go back. If you seemed to feel burdened by your once-loving family, it is time to rekindle the fire of love and concern.

Talk to heaven. Take back the power. Seek the fire. Rekindle the zeal. God is not through with you yet until you finally and quit him.

PRAYER

Father, I am sorry for allowing the fire of zeal to go down. I repent of this attitude and come to you in total surrender to your perfect will. Send down the fire from above and let my life burn with your zeal and holy power once more in the name of Jesus.

SEVEN

I AM GOD'S CHOICE

Acts 1:16
"Brothers," he said, "the Scriptures had to be fulfilled concerning Judas, who guided those who arrested Jesus. This was predicted long ago by the Holy Spirit, speaking through King David.

God can speak from heaven but many times he chooses to speak through his servants. The above chapter is from a prophecy of King David that one day someone will betray the Son of God. Judas Iscariot became the victim of a negative prophecy. Right from the Old Testament to the New Testament, God picked a believer to declare his word and his goodness to humankind. David was one of the few people God chose to speak of wonderful things that would happen in the future.

Looking at his profile, there was nothing special or noble in David. He was a shepherd boy and the last person among many male siblings. God chose him instead and made him one of the most celebrated saints of old. God can use you, speak through you and work wonders through you despite your background. There is always room for one more person in the program of God. Once you realize this and you are willing to be a part, God creates a room big enough to accommodate you. Choose to see God moving and speaking through you

wherever you are right now.
There is no favorite with God.
The humbler your background,
the more glory you bring to his
name. God will make you one of
his best choices right now.

PRAYER
Father, I invoke your grace
upon my life. Pour on me
unmerited favor and divine
appointment. When you make a
choice, no one can change it.
Therefore, I give myself to you;
make me your chosen one from
this moment forward in the
name of Jesus.

EIGHT
I SHALL BE RELEVANT

Acts 2:6
When they heard the loud noise, everyone came running, and they were bewildered to hear their own languages being spoken by the believers.

When the day of Pentecost came, great things took place. One of the remarkable things was the ability to speak in languages previously unlearned. Peter and the other apostles and disciples received a power that was to shake the world. The Holy Spirit came on them and they could speak clearly to the understanding of the many foreigners who gathered to see what was going on. What Peter and other believers were saying meant something to the people. It touched them, changed them, and brought them into the kingdom of God. If their words were not relevant, the people could not have been attracted to God.

You need relevance to make an impact on your family, job, and business. People and things do not respond because you are human. You need to understand how to communicate with them and learn their language if you must get their attention. Your primary assignment as a believer is to touch the people around you. If you cannot speak a language they understand emotionally, psychologically, and mentally, you may be wasting your time. Seek to be relevant through the grace of God to fulfill what the Bible says in Romans 8:19. God's entire creation waits for your manifestation. You must believe it to see it work out in your local church, family, job, business, and personal life.

PRAYER

Father, pour your Spirit on me and upon your people. Make me relevant to myself, to the church, and to the people I meet every day. Let believers like me rise to the needs of the times. Make us relevant in every way until the world knows how great you are.

NINE

THIS IS AMAZING!

Acts 2:12
They stood there amazed and perplexed. "What can this mean?" they asked each other.

The events surrounding Pentecost continues to stun most of us. It is normal for the people who gathered to see what was happening to the followers of Christ to have wondered the same way. When God shows up in your life, everyone will see it, know it, and share in it. Since the world began, no one has ever spoken in tongues. People learned Hebrew and Aramaic but no one has ever spoken a language without learning it first.

The day of Pentecost changed everything. The people saw what they never saw before. They heard what they never heard before and were never in doubt that only God could do those things.

If God has done something for you in the past, do not think that he is done with you. You are yet to see many of the things he can do. And God is yet to show you many more things you do not know is possible. Do not stop expecting bigger things no matter how long it had taken since you last saw God's wonders. God will do something in your life that your spouse and close friends will scream with joy and wonder. Are you ready for those miracles?

PRAYER

Father, work in my life in ways that people around me will wonder in amazement. I desire to see your name glorified everywhere I go. I ask that you pour the miraculous grace of amazing things on my life in the name of Jesus.

TEN

I AM NOT ALONE

Acts 2:14
Then Peter stepped forward
with the eleven other apostles
and shouted to the crowd,
"Listen carefully, all of you,
fellow Jews and residents of
Jerusalem! Make no mistake
about this.

Miracles always follow you
when you receive the Holy
Spirit's power. The people who
came to see what was
happening could not believe
their eyes. They wondered how
a group of Hebrew men and
women could speak their
dialects and languages. It was a
glorious and positive replay of
the incident at the Tower of

Babel. God chose to reveal his glory in different languages that day. When the people inquired to know what was up, Peter came out to make an explanation. As he walked up, the other eleven stood with him.

The remarkable thing about this bold move of Peter was that he was not alone in the fight to defend the faith. He had the support and companionship of the eleven and that must have boosted his confidence. You know how it feels to be alone in a cause. When something needs attention in your workplace, trying to set it right alone may be extremely difficult. But when you have the support of the management, it is easier to get it done.

If you are the pastor of a local church, the support of your members goes a long way to encourage you. More than that, you need God to stand by you through the thick and thin of life.

PRAYER
Father, I repent of the spirit of self-centeredness and I release myself to you. Let me never be alone in a righteous cause. Stand by me and move the right people to stand with me. I receive the same anointing Peter had on the day of Pentecost in the name of Jesus.

ELEVEN

SEE THE EVIDENCE

Acts 2:16
No, what you see was predicted long ago by the prophet Joel:

Peter didn't run out of words when he explained the events of Pentecost to the interested crowd. He was filled with the Holy Spirit already and had no fear. He had the answer and the people were eager to listen. The answer they were looking for was right before their eyes. The Holy Ghost had come and things happened exactly the way it was prophesied in the Book of Joel.

Peter just pointed the crowd to the manifestation of the spirit.

He had come upon the believers and the things the people saw and heard were enough evidence of the truth of God's promises. You need this kind of miracles in your life. You need this kind of miracle in your workplace. You need this kind of miracle in your family and marriage. God does things that people will see and wonder how that was possible in the first place. You have to show them and let them see things themselves and give you feedback whether it was God or man who did such great miracles.

May you receive special miracles that will make you speak less and show more of the goodness of God in the land of the living.

PRAYER

Father, perform special miracles, signs, and wonders in my life that only showing will be enough for doubters and haters to see and believe. I receive this kind of testimony in my life, family, ministry, business, and workplace in the name of Jesus.

TWELVE

IS THIS POSSIBLE?

Acts 2:22-￼23￼
"People of Israel, listen! God publicly endorsed Jesus the Nazarene by doing powerful miracles, wonders, and signs through him, as you well know. But God knew what would happen, and his prearranged plan was carried out when Jesus was betrayed. With the help of lawless Gentiles, you nailed him to a cross and killed him.

The above text tells of the power of God in raising Jesus Christ from the dead. The Roman soldiers and the hating Jews thought they had given him the final blow but God raised His Son on the third day. It was like a dream that even the disciples of Jesus found it hard to believe. No one had this privilege in the past and how could Jesus, a Jew like them, have this special experience? It seemed impossible that Jesus rose from the dead, and Peter could not contain his joy in telling the crowd this good news.

What are you going through in life at the moment? Is your situation hopeless in every way? Do you think there is no remedy to your problem? Have you found yourself in a big mess that you have accepted that nothing can be done to save you? If Jesus conquered death, there is nothing he cannot help you conquer. If death could not keep Jesus inside the grave, nothing can keep you down or throw you off.

While on the cross, Jesus brought every power, curse, bondage, evil, sickness, poverty, and suffering on their knees. He stripped Satan of his power from that day forward. Satan can only bark or roar but true believers know he's just acting it up. He is forever defeated and he knows that. So whatever is keeping you down is breaking the law of freedom in Christ. It is an illegal act and is subject to divine punishment. Say no to illegal tumors, cancer, hypertension, and poverty by rebuking them in the name of Jesus.

PRAYER

Father, Jesus made me your
child by his death on the cross
and through his resurrection. I
declare myself free from all the
illegal occupants and
tormentors in my life. I
command them to go and never
return in the name of Jesus.

THIRTEEN

SEE GOD'S WONDERS

Exodus 14:30-31
That is how the Lord rescued
Israel from the hand of the
Egyptians that day. And the
Israelites saw the bodies of the
Egyptians washed up on the
seashore. When the people of
Israel saw the mighty power
that the Lord had unleashed
against the Egyptians, they
were filled with awe before him.
They put their faith in the Lord
and in his servant Moses.

God saved the Israelites from
the evil rule of Egypt. The
people of God suffered for more
than four hundred years and

cried to God for deliverance. God heard their prayers and sent Moses to lead them out of Egypt. Though the Egyptians thought Israelites were never going to be free, God showed them wonders so great that they knew there was a God in heaven.

Is there anyone or anything holding you captive? Are you struggling with some bad habits? Have you sought promotion, progress, and prosperity and nothing seemed to happen? Just as the Israelites saw God's deliverance, you will see the wonders of God in your life, family, business, and job in Jesus' name.

God will not only force your enemies to set you free, he will terminate their contract, stop their rule and make them as good as dead. They will no longer be a threat to you in any way. You will live your life to the full and have no reasons to fear. The Israelites knew that day that God was with them and always had their back. You may have thought that God is no longer interested in your situation. That is not true. God always used the enemies of his people to demonstrate His awesome power. Who or what has been on your trail for the past week, month or year? You shall see God's wonders as he troubles them until they let you go free to clinch your promotion and success in the name of Jesus.

PRAYER

Father, use the intentions of my enemies to show your wonders in my life. Turn all their evil agenda into a means to glorify your name and to demonstrate your power for all to see in the name of Jesus.

FOURTEEN

YOU SHALL SING A NEW SONG

Exodus 15:1-2
Then Moses and the people of Israel sang this song to the Lord: "I will sing to the Lord, for he has triumphed gloriously; he has hurled both horse and rider into the sea. The Lord is my strength and my song; he has given me victory. This is my God, and I will praise him— my father's God, and I will exalt him!

The many years of bondage did not give the Israelites time to compose and sing any songs of joy. Their lives were filled with sorrow and pain, and their captors cared little of their happiness. Even when they complained, they got more work as a deterrent to future complaints. They were to serve without any protest whatsoever. These robbed them of the peace and joy necessary for songs and thanksgiving to God.

It is the spiritual duty of God's people to sing songs of praise to God. Singing does more in your life than you think. The Israelites knew that so they longed for the day when they would be free to praise and worship their Creator. Does this sound like you? Do you have a situation that has drained your joy and sapped your happiness?

The good news is that God knows where you are and what

you are going through at the moment. Nothing has ever happened in the universe without his knowing. Just as he set the time Israelites' suffering will end, he has set a date for the end of your bondage. As he delivered his people and they sang a new song in his name, so you will be delivered to sing of your deliverance. God will set you free today. He will give you a new song.

PRAYER

Father, today I place an expiration date on every negative situation I am going through in the name of Jesus. I begin to enter my season of joy, peace, happiness, and songs of praise to you. Thank you for putting a new song in my mouth in the name of Jesus.

FIFTEEN

ENEMIES MUST SINK

Exodus 15:5-6

The deep waters gushed over them; they sank to the bottom like a stone. "Your right hand, O Lord, is glorious in power. Your right hand, O Lord, smashes the enemy.

The Egyptians are metaphorically described as stones in the text because of their unpleasant experience. Regardless of size or beauty, a stone sinks to the bottom of the sea. This means that like stones, the Egyptians were already destined to sink to their destruction. Your enemy has been destined to fail the moment they chose to go after you. You are not the one who made it so; God made it that anyone who comes after his children will fail and sink.

The Red Sea was ready to take in the stubborn enemies of God's people. It was a faithful servant of God and so are all things God created. When God chooses to deal with your enemy, nothing can stand in his way. When he wants to destroy anything for your sake, no one can change that. When the enemy falls, they become stones and can never float or rise to challenge you again.

God will silence all your enemies and those who need to sink will go down in disgrace.

Do not try to stop God's
judgment on your enemy. God
knows what he is doing. You
may forgive them, pity them,
but do not attempt to stop God
unless he tells you to intervene
on their behalf. May God dash
all your enemies to pieces and
set you up for great blessings in
the name of Jesus.

PRAYER
Father, I ask that my enemies
be made to sink to the bottom
of the sea. Turn them into
stones and make them too
heavy to float or rise again. And
with their downfall so go all
their evils plans against my life
and progress in the name of
Jesus Christ.

SIXTEEN

RECOVER YOUR LOSS

2 Kings 6:5-6

But as one of them was cutting a tree, his ax head fell into the river. "Oh, sir!" he cried. "It was a borrowed ax!" "Where did it fall?" the man of God asked. When he showed him the place, Elisha cut a stick and threw it into the water at that spot. Then the ax head floated to the surface.

The sons of the prophet noticed that their space was too small for the company. They suggested Prophet Elisha and it was a good one. Elisha gave his consent and the trainee prophets started work right away. While one of them was using an ax, the head of the ax pulled off and fell into the river. He cried and ran to tell Elisha. The powerful prophet inquired after how it happened. Finally, by the word of the prophet, the ax head floated and the man picked it up and went back to work.

The story contains many lessons. Just as the ax was borrowed, you may have taken a loan from your bank or a trusted friend. The business didn't succeed and the capital had sunk into the business and there is nothing to show for the huge investment. Paying back has become impossible and you can only cry like the son of the prophet in our text. Even with a word of prophecy from your pastor, a business venture can go south. Only God knows what tomorrow holds and that is why your faith in God should grow stronger every day.

But one thing to keep in mind is that your lost ax will float again. Your crumbled business will come back to life and you will regain your place in your line of business. Even if you lost your promotion or job interview, you will get them back in the name of Jesus. Don't doubt the power of God. The ax head was made of iron yet it floated. There is nothing impossible with God. He will do it for you, your family, business, job, marriage, kids, and ministry in the name of Jesus.

PRAYER

Father, I open my heart to receive a clear prophecy on my life, family, marriage, business, job, and ministry in the name of Jesus. Let everything in my life that has drowned through carelessness float again in the name of Jesus.

SEVENTEEN
MY ENEMIES WILL FALL

Exodus 15:9-10
"The enemy boasted, 'I will chase them and catch up with them. I will plunder them and consume them. I will flash my sword; my powerful hand will destroy them.' But you blew with your breath, and the sea covered them. They sank like lead in the mighty waters.

When God delivered Israel from Egypt, the Egyptians refused to give up. They chased the Israelites down to the Red Sea. Little did they know that they were helping God to plan their downfall. The Egyptian soldiers saw the people walking through the Red Sea and thought they could do the same thing. It was a mistake that cost their lives. The standing walls of water on both sides merged and swallowed up the frightened soldiers. They knew too late that the God of Israel was alive.

Before their thoughtless pursuit, they boasted that no one could escape from them. Their boastings were in vain the moment they met a Greater Power. Your enemies will fall and never rise again. No matter how hard they come after you and you cannot have a good night's sleep, their mission will fail. Do not be afraid of the enemy in the family or workplace. Your God is stronger than the enemy. He has pronounced judgment on the enemy and they will fall before they know it. God will close them up in the confusion that cannot go away until the last one falls and rise no more.

PRAYER

Father, I ask that all the enemies fall and rise no more in the name of Jesus. Send your wind of judgment and put them in a state of confusion until none is left standing in the name of Jesus.

EIGHTEEN

I WILL REACH MY GOAL

Exodus 15:16-□17□
Terror and dread fall upon
them. The power of your arm
makes them lifeless as stone
until your people pass by, O
Lord, until the people you
purchased pass by. You will
bring them in and plant them
on your own mountain— the
place, O Lord, reserved for your
own dwelling, the sanctuary, O
Lord, that your hands have
established.

The text is a song of victory that
recognized what God did to
save the Israelites from slavery
in Egypt. It is a song that

indicates what happens to the enemy of God's people when God chooses to bless his own. God put the fear of the Israelites on all the nations they passed on their way to the Promised Land. They were unable to harm the Israelites as they journeyed to the place God prepared for them. The enemies became frozen like stones and could do nothing until the people of God walked through their countries.

No matter the evil intentions of the enemy, you will walk into your promotion in the name of Jesus. God never goes to sleep and he will watch over you until you reach your goal. Stop having any fear of the enemy. They are the ones who should fear you. Already they are afraid of you and cannot harm you. Move on, climb higher and reach toward your next big level and watch how God silences all the enemies in the name of Jesus.

PRAYER
Father, I remove every hindrance in my path of success in the name of Jesus. Put fear in the hearts of all enemies so that they will not stand in my way of think of harming me in any way. I receive the anointing to get to my new breakthroughs in the name of Jesus.

NINETEEN

FAVOR IN UNFAMILIAR PLACES

Exodus 15:17
You will bring them in and plant them on your own mountain— the place, O Lord, reserved for your own dwelling, the sanctuary, O Lord, that your hands have established.

Times come when you feel unprepared to take up new challenges and push yourself to limits. It is natural to feel that way but you need to keep in mind that you are the child of the Great King. Others may have limitations and get discouraged by them, but you are different. The lack of confidence can come as a result of experience or a natural aversion to new things. The Israelites had the same challenge. They had been in bondage in Egypt for a long time that they forgot what it was like to be free to choose the best. They did not see themselves qualified enough to get the best of what God had promised them.

God needed to work together with his people to establish them in the Promised Land. In the same way, God will help you feel belonging in that new position you are aspiring to. Never think it is impossible to get there. Others may complain of inadequacy and lack of preparation but you know that your God specializes in impossibilities. He delights in doing things that are natural and scientifically impossible. If your organization has offered you a new appointment, instead of rejecting the offer, accept it and ask God to establish you. God will do it for you beyond your experience and available skills in the name of Jesus.

PRAYER

Father, you have promised to establish me in my inheritance. I ask that you do according to your word. In the name of Jesus, I overcome fear, doubt, and anything that wants to rob me of my newfound success. Grant me access and success at every level you take me in the name of Jesus Christ.

TWENTY

FROM BITTER TO SWEET

Exodus 15:22-25

Then Moses led the people of Israel away from the Red Sea, and they moved out into the desert of Shur. They traveled in this desert for three days without finding any water. When they came to the oasis of Marah, the water was too bitter to drink. So they called the place Marah (which means "bitter"). Then the people complained and turned against Moses. "What are we going to drink?" they demanded. So Moses cried out to the Lord for help, and the Lord showed him a piece of wood. Moses threw it into the water, and this made the water good to drink. It was there at Marah that the Lord set before them the following decree as a standard to test their faithfulness to him.

It is natural to murmur and complain when we do not see any hope ahead. The Israelites had some experiences that tried their patience to breaking point. They walked for miles without food and water. As humans, there right to speak of their deprivations. However, as children of God, they were supposed to trust God who had brought them out of Egypt. If God was able to do the first things, he was also able to do the remaining. But their hunger and thirst were so great that the Israelites did not remember

how powerful and caring God
was.

Luckily, God was merciful to
them and instructed Moses to
do something spectacular. The
only water they found on their
journey at that time was bitter.
God told Moses what to do to
make the water sweet and
normal for His people. Others
might drink that water and get
a bitter experience but God's
people will always have a sweet
experience with it. One thing is
important here: Moses listened
to God's instructions and a
miracle took place. If he had
paid no attention, many would
have died of the bitter water.
Thank God Moses was a man
who had learned to listen to the
voice of God.

Is there any bitter situation in your life, relationship, or workplace? Are you having a terrible experience with your spouse or teenage kids? Does your employer make life bitter for you almost every day? A specific instruction from God can put an end to all your worries. But you have to learn to be quiet in God's presence. It is not enough to pray when you cannot wait to hear what God wants you to do. Pray and listen to hear what God will direct you to do from his word. He will give you a specific powerful instruction that will end all the bitter experiences you have in the name of Jesus.

PRAYER

Father, give me a specific instruction that will bring

solutions to my bitter experience in the name of Jesus. Turn the bitterness in my marriage, relationships, business, and workplace to sweetness and fill my life with miracles in the name of Jesus.

BOOKS BY THE AUTHOR

And here's my special GIFT to you.

www.ingramcontent.com/pod-product-compliance
Lightning Source LLC
Chambersburg PA
CBHW051452150726